Seek And Find

Dustin,
 Thank you for being open to reading this.

#14 on page 25 was the one we discussed but there's probably more on the topic.

I hope this is a blessing,
 Beverly

Seek And Find

*A Practical, Barebones, Guide
To Understanding The Obstacles To
And Essentials Of Christianity
And Why I Should Know Them*

written by
BEVERLY SWIMM

Theological Editor, Dr. Curt Morgan

Edited by Bill Callen

Seek And Find: A Practical, Barebones Guide to Understanding The Obstacles To And Essentials Of Christianity And Why I Should Know Them

Copyright © 2015 by Beverly Swimm

All rights reserved. No part of this book may be used or reproduced in any form, electronic or mechanical, including photocopying, recording, or scanning into any information storage and retrieval system, without written permission from the author except in the case of brief quotation embodied in critical articles and reviews.

This book is a project of Seek and Find Ministries

Book design by The Troy Book Makers

Printed in the United States of America
The Troy Book Makers • Troy, New York • thetroybookmakers.com

To order additional copies of this title, contact your favorite local bookstore or visit www.tbmbooks.com

ISBN: 978-1-61468-3155

Introduction

Have you ever thought any or all of the following?

- I'm not into religion.

- Churches only care about money and power.

- Christians are a hateful bunch of hypocrites.

- God has the whole world to deal with; He doesn't have time for me and my problems.

- All good people go to heaven.

- Hell is only for truly evil people.

If so, you're not alone.

God, heaven and hell are sort of like death and taxes – we really don't want to contemplate them until it is absolutely necessary and even then we sometimes have to be dragged into it.

The United States is considered to be a "Christian nation", and most Americans have heard of God, learned about Jesus, and even attended church. If you use to go to church, why did you stop? What do you think of church, Christians and God? Where do your ideas come from? Friends and acquaintances? TV shows, newspapers or some other media?

If you were sick or hurt, would you consult a doctor or the newspapers? If you needed surgery, would you research the procedure or ask your friends about it? And if you needed insight, would you try to understand it from your limited knowledge, look for it on the local news or by speaking to others who have gone through the process? I hope you would agree the wise choices are to speak with a surgeon or two, research the procedure and learn all you could about it because it will affect the rest of your life.

The same approach should be applied to God, Christianity and faith. Don't trust what you hear or read from outside sources, but learn for yourself who God is and what He can mean to you.

In the following pages you will find some basic answers to several common questions and corrections to common misconceptions. Of course, there is always further research and learning to be done – what we have here is a good starting point.

So whether you want to have a better understanding of God, or just a better understanding of those around you, this quick and easy overview will fit your needs.

Maybe you go to church occasionally, perhaps on Christmas and Easter, or even once a month and have faith that God is real. There are topics that will help you to understand God's plan for you and the wonderful opportunities that will come from knowing that plan.

Or maybe you have faith in God yourself and know of someone who is hurting and struggling in life and want him or her to have the same comfort you do but don't know how to relate God's truths to that person. This book offers you the opportunity to learn how to share your beliefs or because it is the basics, you could give it to them to read on their own.

No matter which category best describes you and your situation, this is the perfect starter book.

Acknowledgements

Completing this book has been challenging, but truly rewarding. I would like to thank my children, Katie, Tommy, Joshua and Holly for their encouragement and faith in me.

I would like to acknowledge the many — and I mean MANY — Pastors, teachers, friends, fellow Christians and family whose wisdom and insights were invaluable and inspirational as the project progressed. I am ever so thankful for those who seek to help others grow in their faith.

And most importantly, I give all my praise to God for His forgiveness, first and foremost, but also for the way He has blessed my life with a wonderful family, a dedicated and faithful church and fellow Christians who strive to be God's light for others in this world.

I pray this book will be a blessing to you and those around you.

                                        Sincerely,
                                        Beverly Swimm

In honor of my beloved mother, Betty Smithers and Aunt Jean Cariel who embodied and demonstrated God's love to their family and who's heritage is and will be carried through the generations.

How To Use The Book

There are different ways in which you can use this book. First and most simply, you can read it from front to back. Or second, you can peruse the list of entries in the front to first seek answers to your most pressing questions or concerns. Finally, there is an index in the back arranged by topic, ranging from "Understanding God" to "Character Issues" so that you may find and read all applicable entries about a specific topic at one time.

In addition, this book is designed so that you can read it in one sitting or as slow paced as one entry per day.

No matter which way you prefer, it is my hope and prayer that you will learn this very day exactly what you need to live a blessed life.

Daily Entries

1. I'm Not Into Religion
2. There Are Too Many Rules
3. The Bible Was Written By Man, So Why Should I Believe It?
4. I Don't Want Anyone Telling Me What I Have To Do!
5. Does God Love Me?
6. God Created Each Of Us With A Hole In Our Heart
7. What Is Sin?
8. We Are Born Sinners
9. The Sin That Separates Us From God
10. The Church Would Burn Down If I Stepped Through The Door!
11. God Has A Plan And Purpose For Everyone
12. Definition Of God
13. If God Is Love, Why Is There So Much Pain And Suffering The World?
14. If That's Being A Christian, Count Me Out!
15. God's Mercy
16. I Do More Good Than Bad, So I Should Be Able To Go To Heaven.

17. The Bible Was Written In A Different Time And Therefore Is Not Relevant Now

18. What Is Faith?

19. Does God Answer Prayer?

20. Fear Of God

21. Is Satan Real?

22. Satan's Lie's

23. I Am Not Worthy

24. The Bible Is Too Confusing

25. Church Is Full Of Hypocrites!

26. Don't Worry About Me And God – We Have It Worked Out

27. Does God Speak To Us?

28. God's Blessings

29. Christ's Example

30. My Grandmother Would Turn Over In Her Grave If I Went To That Church!

31. All I Need Is To Be A Good Person

32. Christians Are Some Of The Most Judgmental People I Know!

33. Christians Have An Entitlement Attitude

34. Hell

35. Heaven

36. The Trinity - Father, Son And Holy Spirit

37. You WILL Live Forever!

38. Death Is Nothingness - No Pain, No Memory; It Won't Be So Bad

39. What Does It Mean To Have Joy?

40. If Getting Saved Is So Simple, You Might Ask, Then Why Not Just Wait And Do It On My Deathbed?

1

I'm Not Into Religion

That's great, because neither is God. At least, God is not into 'religion' the way that we interpret that word today.

The word religion is only used 5 times in the King James Version of the Bible. Four of those five times refer to strict Jewish teachings and the fifth is used in reference to assisting widows and orphans:

> Pure religion and undefiled before God and the Father is this, to visit the fatherless and widows in their affliction, and to keep himself unspotted from the world. (James 1:27)

In the Old Testament, there were lots of rules or laws that God's people were required to adhere to, but that was all changed by Jesus' coming to Earth. Nowadays, we use the word 'religion' to quantify all the things we are supposed to do for God, for our church, and for pastors or priests.

But the real truth is that God is into relationships, and not at all into 'religion' the way we perceive it today. He desires a relationship with each of us, which is in fact why he created us. He 'calls' us into fellowship with Him.

> "God is faithful, through whom you were called into fellowship with His Son, Jesus Christ our Lord." (1 Corinthians 1:9)

All religion, my friend, is simply evolved out of fraud, fear, greed, imagination, and poetry.

– Edgar Allan Poe

2
....

There Are Too Many Rules

Most rules in popular religions are not God's intentions for us. Some of these rules include when to sit, stand or kneel, when to go to church, whether to dance and what to do with money. Jesus was asked what 'rules' were important, and thankfully, He gave us a direct answer:

> "Love the Lord your God with all your heart and with all your soul and with all your mind. This is the first and greatest commandment. And the second is like it: Love your neighbor as yourself." (Matthew 22:37-39)

In the Old Testament, God's people were given the 10 Commandments, so that when they are followed, everyone could live in peace with one another. When Christ came, He made it clear that though the commandments are still relevant, the most important rules are to love God and to love each other.

There are many religions that have laws, rules and/or edicts. These may be necessary acts that attendees must complete to reach a level of approval within their "religious" community. Bible-based Christianity, though, is not like that.

The Bible, the Word of God, should be the ultimate authority. If a religious ideology is asking or commanding someone to do certain things or act specific ways, the Bible will articulate whether it is God's design or if it is man-made.

And if the statute is man-made, then it is not under God's authority and no one should be pressured to comply.

> "Since you died with Christ to the elemental spiritual forces of this world, why, as though you still belonged to the world, do you submit to its rules." (Colossians 2:20)

I wish (Christianity) were more productive of good works ... I mean real good works ... not holy day keeping, sermon-hearing ... or making long prayers, filled with flatteries and compliments despised by wise men, and much less capable of pleasing the deity.

— Benjamin Franklin

3

The Bible Was Written By Man, So Why Should I Believe It?

Yes, strictly speaking, the Bible was "written" by man - men 'wrote' the words – but those words were inspired by God. Do you believe in God, who created the heavens and the earth? Well, if He is capable to do that, then He would have to be also capable of relating His story to certain people so that it is written just the way He intended it.

> "And we also thank God continually because, when you received the word of God, which you heard from us, you accepted it not as a human word, but as it actually is, the word of God, which is indeed at work in you who believe." (1 Thessalonians 2:13)

Why should we believe the Bible is actually the word of God? Because, no other book in history comes close to the significance and the uniqueness of the Bible.

The Bible's significance:

- The Bible inspired the invention of the printing press,

- Men devoted their lives to handwriting it,

- It is the most copied book in history, as well as the all-time No.1 best seller and most printed book,

- Many homes have multiple copies,

- It is the most translated book in the world,

- Tens of thousands of books have been written about the Bible,

- Art for centuries centered on the Bible,

- Few other books have been banned by public schools.

The Bible's Uniqueness:

The Bible is a collection of 66 books, written by 40 authors from all walks of life who resided on 3 continents. It was written in three languages and written over 1200 years, yet it is unified in themes, philosophy and content to a mind boggling extent.

Consider a modern day analogy. There's an accident on the road with a few witnesses. Will the accounts of the witnesses be the same or will they vary depending on one's perspective? We know all too well from our jury system that no two people tell the exact same story. Yet, regardless of the many authors, massive geographic regions and hundreds of years, the Bible is amazingly unified in its theme of love and Jesus' redemptive power.

I believe the Bible is the best gift God has ever given to men. All the good from the Savior of the world is communicated to us through this book.

– Abraham Lincoln

4
....

I Don't Want Anyone Telling Me What I Have To Do, Or What I Can And What I Can't Do!

That's understandable - you had enough people telling you what to do when you were a child. As an adult, you're free, on your own and no one can tell you what to do, and if someone does, you don't have to comply.

And thankfully, there's good news for you: God doesn't need you to adhere to others' expectations of you! What he wants is a relationship with you. God wants you to embrace His love for you and for other people, and to make that choice freely, without coercion.

When the requirements and judgment of others determines your state of wellbeing, you could become a 'people pleaser'. The desire for approval could be so strong that a person could easily lose their way spiritually, even if what they are doing seems, on the surface, to be fulfilling a spiritual aim. You may go to church, for example, because that's what others expect of you. You may feel like you have to put money in the offering plate as it passes, or say the right things or stand or kneel at the right time. But God doesn't keep score concerning these 'requirements'. And thankfully, His grace doesn't require a checklist.

> "Their worship is a farce, for they teach man-made ideas as commands from God." (Matthew 15:9)

Yes, God wants you to invest your time with other Christians, to trust Him and to give a portion of your earnings to further the sharing of His Word, but that which God asks — not commands — of you is between you and God, and should not be under the scrutiny of others.

The Bible teaches us not to add or take away anything from God's Word, and that any religion that insists we practice rituals not mentioned in it are outside God's authority and therefore man-made and we are free to avoid them.

Rules are not necessarily sacred, principles are.
– Franklin D. Roosevelt

5
....

Does God Love Me?

God's love for each of us is beyond deep; it is immeasurable. This profound love is tied to His being our Creator.

His love for us is infinite, but because our thinking is finite, we are not able to fully grasp its magnitude. But we can attempt to get a glimpse into God's heart.

Imagine a child in art class. He takes his piece of clay and molds it. He works and reworks it until he is satisfied that it is all he wants it to be. The child seasons it, bakes and paints it. And he loves this finished product, takes care of it, shows it off and is so very proud of it. All this emotion for a mere piece of clay!

Now, how much more do we love our children? Now multiply that astronomically to see a glimpse of God's love for each of us.

Out of this love comes one of the reasons for our creation — so that we may have a relationship with God and for God to accomplish His purposes through us.

"I will praise thee; for I am fearfully and wonderfully made." (Psalm 139:14)

We hold these truths to be self-evident, that all men are created equal, that they are endowed by their Creator with certain unalienable Rights that among these are Life, Liberty and the pursuit of Happiness.

– The Declaration of Independence

6
·······

God Created Each of Us With A Hole In Our Heart

We are searchers. We search for fun, happiness, excitement, a partner, a career, contentment, success, adventure, good health, peace and harmony. We seek these things and often find them — but do we ever feel fully complete? Or do we need a higher-paying job, a little more excitement, a partner who suits us better? Is the peace you enjoyed upon reaching a goal truly lasting?

Think about a jigsaw puzzle. You've spent time and energy placing every piece in its proper place, but you get to the end and discover one piece is missing. You try to plug the gap with something else or paint over the hole, but the truth is, without that piece, the picture is imperfect.

So it is with us. The Bible tells us God created all of us and even knows us by name, but He left out a piece or a gap that only He can fill. Many of us try to fill that void with the things of our world, and though they may give us temporary relief or satisfaction, only God in His rightful place can make us whole.

We have plenty of false gods — 60-hour work weeks; over indulgence in seemingly morally neutral activities like running or golf; and illicit relationships. But only by welcoming God into our hearts can we enjoy a peace that endures, a life that is purposeful and complete, and contentment that is everlasting.

"A person can do nothing better than to eat and drink and find satisfaction in their own toil. . . . for without Him, who can eat or find enjoyment?" (Ecclesiastes 3:24)

And no matter how many pieces of our lives fall away, once we have God in our hearts, the picture will always be complete.

The foundation of the Christian's peace is everlasting; it is what no time, no change can destroy. … The fountain of His comfort shall never be diminished, and the stream shall never be dried. His comfort and joy is a living spring in the soul, a well of water springing up to everlasting life.

– Jonathan Edwards

7
•••••••
What Is Sin?

The dictionary defines sin this way: An act, thought, or way of behaving that goes against the law or teachings of a religion, especially when the person who commits it is aware of this; something that offends a moral or ethical principle.

Let's break this down into three parts.

First, a sin can be an act, like stealing or committing adultery. Second, sin can be a thought, like lust or envy. Third, sin can be a way of behaving, like lying or treating others with abuse or contempt.

In addition, the person's motivations are important to consider. This goes to awareness. When a toddler takes a toy from a playmate, they are portraying no evil intent. But when we steal from others, have inappropriate thoughts, lie to get what we want, or act to accomplish our selfish desires, there is clearly sinful intent.

The third part of the dictionary definition concerns the offensiveness of sin. Who do we offend when we sin? The answer is everyone around us, including ourselves. But most importantly, we offend God.

Sin separates us from God, a division that can be bridged only by God who loves us immeasurably, but who hates sin just as deeply.

> "Your (God's) eyes are too pure to look on evil; you cannot tolerate wrongdoing." (Habakkuk 1:13)

So, why do we sin, and what are the earthly consequences of sin? Why we sin is the easier question: Hebrews 11:25 tells us that "there are pleasures in sin for a season".

The earthly consequences of sin include guilt, shame, chaos, pain and troubled relationships. What a terrible way to live - but that's nothing compared to the eternal significance of sin:

"For the wages of sin is death …" (Romans 6:23a)

But take heart; the second half of that verse brings victory:

" . . . but the gift of God is eternal life through Jesus Christ our Lord." (Romans 6:23b)

The Bible will keep you from sin, or sin will keep you from the Bible.

– Dwight L. Moody

8
....
We Are Born Sinners

Some people like to say humans are "basically good," or that we have an innate or natural inclination toward goodness. If you believe that, I challenge you to sit in a room with a few toddlers and observe their interaction.

You already know what you will see: selfishness, anger, frustration.

Parents have to teach their children morals and ethics: to share, to be kind and to obey. If children were naturally good, we'd have to teach them to lie and to be selfish, which obviously isn't the case. Unfortunately, we have to conclude that we are born sinful.

Our instincts are selfish and to behave in such a way as to further our own agendas. We lie, cheat and steal because somewhere inside, we believe it benefits us. That "somewhere inside" is the problem. We are not liars because we lie; we lie because, at our core, we are liars.

It's like a golden cantaloupe picked from the garden to sit all day in the sun. It still looks good on the outside, but inside it is rotten.

As the New Testament letter to the Romans reminds us (from The Message Bible) Romans 5:12: "You know the story of how Adam landed us in the dilemma we're in — first sin, then death, and no one exempt from either sin or death. That sin disturbed relations with God in everything and everyone . . ."

And in Ephesians 2: "We all did it, all of us doing what

we felt like doing, when we felt like doing it, all of us in the same boat. It's a wonder God didn't lose his temper and do away with the whole lot of us. Instead, immense in mercy and with an incredible love, he embraced us. He took our sin-dead lives and made us alive in Christ. He did all this on his own, with no help from us!"

We cannot fix the sinful part of us on our own, but we do have our part in it. God sent His Son for us. Jesus' death and resurrection fixed it for us – our part is to believe it!

One leak will sink a ship, and one sin will destroy a sinner.
– John Bunyan

9
·······

God and Sin
The Sin That Separates Us

God created each of us and loves us as unique individuals. And God desires a relationship with us, but there's a roadblock — sin.

God is everything that is pure and holy. He hates sin because it goes against His perfect nature. He can't look at sin; therefore, He can't look at us in our natural, sinful state.

Take a moment to consider what you find horrifying. What, for you, is so disgusting that you have to look away? For some it is spoiled milk, for others, perhaps the sight of blood, or a dead animal on the street. The typical evening newscast gives most people plenty to turn away from. Each person has his or her own examples of horrific sights, specific to them.

For God, <u>all</u> sin is revolting. He can't stand the sight of it. This would be really bad news for us, except that God has a plan to knock down this roadblock.

From Romans 3, in The Message, "God sacrificed Jesus on the altar of the world to clear that world of sin. Having faith in him sets us in the clear. God decided on this course of action in full view of the public — to set the world in the clear with Himself through the sacrifice of Jesus, finally taking care of the sins He had so patiently endured."

The good news is this: Once a person has believed by faith that Christ's death on the cross was for their own forgiveness of sins, it's as if Christ is standing between God and the person's sin, and He will no longer hold it against us.

I am a most noteworthy sinner, but I have cried out to the Lord for grace and mercy, and they have covered me completely. I have found the sweetest consolation since I made it my whole purpose to enjoy His marvellous Presence.

– Christopher Columbus

10
·······

The Church Would Burn Down If I Stepped Through The Door!

You can relax if you even theoretically believe this. There have been no breaking news bulletins about a church spontaneously combusting because the world's biggest sinner just stepped through the doors.

Unfortunately, it's not unusual for people to have strong feelings of guilt and unworthiness manifested in self-talk along the lines of "I'm not good enough." God says in the Bible that there is nothing "new under the sun." The same sin that existed in Biblical days is still around today. God has seen it all - every sin, every diabolical act and every betrayal, and is ready to forgive it all. He is greater and more full of grace than all the sin in the world. There is no sin He doesn't already know you've committed and that He will not forgive when you ask Him to.

God wants you to have a blessed life and He doesn't want you to live in sin, but that doesn't mean that He'd have lightening strike a church upon your presence.

> "But he said to me, 'My grace is sufficient for you, for my power is made perfect in weakness.' Therefore I will boast all the more gladly about my weaknesses, so that Christ's power may rest on me." (2 Corinthians 12:9)

No one is "good enough," but God's grace is sufficient to forgive all of our sins.

Grace is free sovereign favor to the ill-deserving.
– Benjamin Warfield

11

God Has A Plan And Purpose For Everyone

Like the subject of an artist's painting, God has a picture of us in His mind, and He wants to bring that vision to canvas.

God's image of each one of us is based on how He designed us – each of us, uniquely. We are a sketch, and we have to allow our Painter to work on and perfect us.

God gave each of us different talents, abilities and passions. When we find the place where these things intersect, we will have found our calling. And when we find and fulfill that calling, we will also find the best life possible.

Recognizing our purpose can be a long journey, but it will be the best journey we will ever take. Remember though, that our world needs plumbers, painters, bankers as well as missionaries, and if we choose to be a missionary when our true calling is to be a mechanic, though our ministry may be blessed, we certainly are not fulfilling our highest purpose.

> "Thy word is a lamp unto my feet and a light unto my path." (Psalm 119:105)

God gives us light so we know the path to follow.

If God is your partner, make your plans BIG!
— D.L. Moody

12
....

Definition Of God

Let's start with the answer in Westminster Shorter Catechism's question: What is God?

"God is a Spirit, infinite, eternal, and unchangeable, in His being, wisdom, power, holiness, justice, goodness, and truth."

You've heard it said that God is love. The true meaning of that fact is worthy of our consideration and reflection.

When someone "loves" another person or even an activity or object, they make choices that affirm this love. For example, someone who "loves" his vehicle will show the world by the way it sparkles and maybe even by it being parked sideways in the back of a parking lot.

Our focus and energy tend to be on that which we love the most, whether that's an object, an activity or a person. Someone who loves to play golf and looks forward to his weekly matches with friends will spend his free time at the driving range, hoping to perfect his game.

Like in relationships, a woman who loves her husband and children will encourage them, play with them and care for them. She does these things to ensure their well-being because of her love for them. And a well-loved person will be joyful, caring and happy.

Now imagine how God's characteristics are manifested from His love.

"And so we know and rely on the love God has for us. God is love." (1 John 4:16)

He is compassionate.

"It is of the LORD's mercies that we are not consumed, because his compassions fail not." (Lamentations 3:22)

He is forgiving.

"And be ye kind one to another, tenderhearted, forgiving one another, even as God for Christ's sake hath forgiven you." (Ephesians 4:32)

He is full of grace.

"And he passed in front of Moses, proclaiming, 'The LORD, the LORD, the compassionate and gracious God, slow to anger, abounding in love and faithfulness …'" (Exodus 34:6)

God is everything we need Him to be, and if we trust in Him, He will show His love to us in a mighty way.

In math, if you divide an infinite number by any number, no matter how large, you still have an infinite quotient. So Jesus' love, being infinite, even though it is divided up for every person on earth, is still infinitely poured out on each one of us!
– C.H. Spurgeon

13
....

If God Is Love, Why Is There So Much Pain And Suffering In The World?

Unfortunately, there is no all-inclusive or easy answer to this popular question. There are tragedies and trials that we will never be able to understand while we are on Earth. But there are some truths that we can cling to.

God is faithful; He has proved how much He loves us and desires to spend eternity with us. In addition, God gives us understanding and wisdom when we most need it. The Bible says in Roman 8:28, "All things work together for good for those who love God." Knowing this, we can have faith that God knows what is best, and therefore we can rest and have peace in His ability to ultimately bring out His goodness in any situation.

We are able to discern the origins of some tragedies, however. Sin is the most common reason for the pain and suffering we bare. God gives all of us free will, and too often we choose to sin or tragically suffer the results of other's sinful choices.

We know that every action has a consequence, even if it's done in secret. Lying results in broken relationships. Sexual immorality leads to disease and heartache. Adultery devastates families. The list is endless.

God allows us to suffer these consequences because they will be for our ultimate good. We learn lessons so that we don't repeat our mistakes, and are also able to caution others.

As mere humans, we will not know all the answers, but

we must trust that God's ways are higher and better than ours. We don't have the capacity to always understand why we suffer and endure pain; but God knows the past, present and the future and desires good outcomes for us. We may not always see the "good" referred to in the verse below, but God is worthy of our faith in Him and we can trust in His goodness.

> "And we know that all things work together for good to them that love God ..." (Romans 8:28)

Once you look at the cross, you can't look at anything else, no matter how horrid it appears, and infer that God's intention is to do us harm. The truth is that God is good.
— William Backcus

14

If That's Being A Christian, Count Me Out!

God's greatest commandments are to love the Lord and to love your neighbor. If so-called Christians are not acting according to those two commandments, then, of course, you don't want any part of them. They act like hypocrites.

But please know that they are sinners, fallen short of Jesus' perfect example of how to live, just like everyone else. Christians make mistakes, choose unwisely and have bad attitudes. And yes, sometimes they aren't pleasant to be around. That doesn't change their destination, though; it just indicates how much further they have to travel on their journey towards emulating Christ and therefore being who God wants them to be.

These Christians aren't good role models for sure. Not now, anyway. But don't let a flawed Christian's poor example cause you to miss out on all of the wonderful things God has planned for you. Don't let the sins of others stop you from having a relationship with God and reaping the benefits of that bond.

And remember to give grace to others (cut them some slack), just as we need that same grace (slack) ourselves.

> "Jesus replied: 'Love the Lord your God with all your heart and with all your soul and with all your mind. This is the first and greatest commandment. And the second is like it: Love your neighbor as yourself.'" (Matthew 22:37-39)

Hypocrites in the Church? Yes, and in the lodge and at the home. Don't hunt through the Church for a hypocrite. Go home and look in the mirror. Hypocrites? Yes. See that you make the number one less.

– Billy Sunday

15

God's Mercy

"I throw myself on the mercy of the court!"

Why would someone say that? Because they realize they are guilty, they have been caught and recognize that their punishment is coming, though they are hopeful it will be less harsh than what they know they deserve.

This analogy is a great example of the basic definition of mercy: "kindness or forgiveness shown especially to somebody a person has power over; a disposition to be compassionate or forgiving of others."

In short, mercy is undeserved forgiveness or withholding of a deserved punishment.

God knows we are going to mess up, make mistakes, and make unwise choices, but He is ready and willing to forgive us when we repent because Christ received the punishment our sins deserve. God displays His mercy in His forgiveness.

In Psalm 156, all 26 verses end with "His mercy endures forever." This is great news for us because we are going to live forever, and we can have faith and trust that God's mercy is endless.

> "For as the heaven is high above the earth, so great is his mercy toward them that fear him." (Psalm 103:11)

I have always found that mercy bears richer fruits than strict justice.
– Abraham Lincoln

16
. . . .

I Do More Good Than Bad, So I Should Be Able To Go To Heaven

Attempting to constantly keep the scales tipped in your favor must be a very burdensome way to live. Living in wonder would carry an incredible amount of stress: heaven — "Will or won't I make it there?"

In reality, it took only one sin for you to be guilty in God's eyes, and that probably happened before you even could conceivably have a memory of it. Consider this simple but familiar example: Disobedience to your parents is sin, so if you were told not to take a toy from another child and you did it anyway, you are guilty. And if you are a normal American, that was only the start of a lengthy list of sins accumulated in your life.

Thankfully, living for eternity in heaven is not determined by the good or bad things we do in this life. We actually should appreciate that. How difficult would it be to continually examine our lives, constantly trying to balance our deeds and misdeeds?

God doesn't want you to waste the life He has given you with such harmful uncertainty anyways. He made it easy for us!

> "For by grace are ye saved through faith; and that not of yourselves: it is the gift of God. Not of works, lest any man should boast." (Ephesians 2:8)

The good news is that it's not about our goodness or

"works" in contrast to our sins; it doesn't matter if we've committed one sin or a thousand; whether we've lied or committed murder, the imbalance is the same. Consider the scales:

We can heap every sin that we have committed and ever will commit onto one side and Christ will do more than balance out the weight; He will remove the scales completely.

"As far as the east is from the west, so far hath He removed our transgressions from us." (Psalms 103:12)

God is capable of wiping our slates clean and separating us as far from our sins as the east is from the west.

The Gospel is good news of mercy to the undeserving. The symbol of the religion of Jesus is the cross, not the scales.
— John R. W. Stott

17

The Bible Was Written In A Different Time And Therefore Is Not Relevant Now

Is it true that something written chronicling life long ago has no bearing on our modern times? Are our times so different that the issues and themes captured in the Bible are no longer applicable?

Let's examine the character issues that King David (also the David of the Goliath story), who lived thousands of years ago, struggled with.

David was selfish, lied, coveted another man's wife, committed adultery and murder, was grief stricken and survived the death of his son. David felt guilt, remorse, vulnerability, lust, love and shame, just to name a few emotions with which he had to deal. David speaks about all of these things in the Bible.

Do you still think the Bible isn't relevant? In these modern days, people struggle with the same problems that plagued David's life. Thankfully though, he described his troubles, and how God helped him endure and overcome them. The words and testimony of David offer us assurance that God is ready, willing and able to help us today if we are humble enough to ask for it.

> "What has been will be again, what has been done will be done again; there is nothing new under the sun." (Ecclesiastes 1:9)

There is nothing new under the sun. David dealt with

issues that still burden us today – the times really aren't so different after all.

It is impossible to enslave mentally or socially a Bible-reading people. The principles of the Bible are the groundwork of human freedom.

– Horace Greeley

18

What Is Faith?

Keep the faith! We hear this often when our efforts are falling short. It has become a kind of shorthand; when we hear it, we know someone is encouraging us to continue to believe, regardless of our current status.

The dictionary defines faith in several ways: strong or unshakeable belief in something, especially without proof or evidence; trust in God and in His actions and promises; a conviction of the truth of certain doctrines of religion, especially when this is not based on reason.

The Bible describes faith this way:

> "Now faith is the substance of things hoped for, the evidence of things not seen." (Hebrews 11:1)

To put it plainly, faith is 'believing without seeing'.

We all have faith in something: our jobs, other people, money, the economy, our government. Unfortunately, none of these things is worthy of our faith. A job can be lost. People will disappoint us. Our money can disappear in the stock market. Governments change, and many times not for the better. Some people have faith in themselves, imagining they can control their destiny.

They cannot however. But God can, and does.

> "… for He hath said, I will never leave you, nor forsake you." (Hebrews 13:5)

God promised us that He would never leave us. The riches of the world can vanish in an instant, but God's promises endure. He alone, the Creator and Giver of all good things, is worthy of our trust, our faith and our lives.

Faith is taking the first step even when you don't see the whole staircase.

–Martin Luther King, Jr.

19
....

Does God Answer Prayer?

Yes — God always answers prayer. But we must understand that God's answer isn't always 'yes'.

As parents, we are asked, implored and pleaded with to comply with the requests of our children. Sometimes our reply is quick and easy, but many times our contemplation can be long, especially if we want to avoid saying no. But we have to make tough choices because we see a bigger picture that our children often cannot.

This is how it is with our requests of God. He absolutely sees the big picture; actually, He sees the whole picture, and just because we want, desire or believe that we need something, that doesn't necessarily mean it is what is best for us and our situation.

And God does not always answer us in black and white. Sometimes, He wants us to wait, to learn and grow so that when He does respond, we are better able to contend with His answer, regardless of the outcome.

But the most important point is that we can have faith in God's promise that He hears our prayers.

> "Then you will call on me and come and pray to me, and I will listen to you." (Jeremiah 29:12)

Our prayers should be for blessings in general, for God knows best what is good for us.
– Socrates

20
....

Fear Of God

"Be not wise in thine own eyes: fear the LORD, and depart from evil." (Proverbs 3:7)

Why does God want us to fear him?

Fear: An unpleasant feeling of anxiety or apprehension caused by the presence or anticipation of danger.

We know God does not want us to have anxiety, so where is this danger coming from? Consider the following situation:

Gary, the sales manager, hired John to work on his team because of his passion and strong work ethic. He trained and mentored John and encouraged him along the way. John responded and performed admirably for the company.

One day, a vendor of the company offered John a weekend away at a nearby resort as a thank you for the recent increase in purchases. Even though some sales people privately accepted such opportunities, to do so was against company policy. John declined the offer — fear of damaging his relationship with his mentor and dishonoring his boss made it an easy choice for him.

This is the same fear God desires from us. He wants us to make good and honest choices and fear losing His respect. Besides, if we fear God then we need not fear anything else!

". . . fear of the Lord is the beginning of wisdom."
(Psalm 111:10)

A concise definition of what it means to fear God: the acute awareness of the presence of God's power that produces in me sense of awe and calls forth from me honor, respect and reverence.

– Graham Paddock

21

Is Satan Real?

Satan wants you to believe he is not real. But, he is very real and has very specific intentions toward each of us. Contrary to popular beliefs, though, his ultimate goal is not for us to be bad or to do bad things.

You've heard the saying "the devil made me do it," or visualized an angel on one shoulder and a devil on the other, competing for your attention. Yes, Satan revels in our poor decisions but they are not his end game; his purpose is far more destructive — our ultimate and eternal separation from God.

God created Satan, though at that time he was known as Lucifer (meaning light or angel of light), to be in fellowship with Him. Later, Lucifer equated himself with God and, filled with pride, led a rebellion against Him. The consequence of Satan's rebellion was that he was cast out of God's presence along with his angels, who we now refer to as demons.

And now Satan wants that same fate for us, and is willing to use any means necessary to achieve his goal.

> "Be alert and of sober mind. Your enemy the devil prowls around like a roaring lion looking for someone to devour." (1 Peter 5:8)

But fear not, because Christ is greater than the devil:

> "Ye are of God, little children, and have overcome them: because greater is he (Christ) that is in you, than he (Satan) that is in the world." (1 John 4:4)

No one is a firmer believer in the power of prayer than the devil; not that he practices it, but he suffers from it.

– Gary H. King

22
....

Satan's Lie's

Satan is a liar. He will do his best to make you believe whatever is necessary to achieve his ultimate goal for you: your eternal separation from God.

> "… He was a murderer from the beginning, not holding to the truth, for there is no truth in him. When he lies, he speaks his native language, for he is a liar and the father of lies." (John 8:44)

This is just a small sampling of Satan's lies that have unfortunately taken root in many lives:

- Life is short!

- You deserve to enjoy yourself.

- You are worthless.

- It's ok, you're only telling a little lie.

- You are strong and can handle all of life's difficulties by yourself.

- Fulfilling your sinful desires is the most you can hope from this life.

Humans have experienced these lies since the beginning of time. Adam and Eve were the first to encounter Satan's falsehoods, and to this day, Satan continues to use the same tactics.

Thankfully, we don't have to believe any of them. God's Word addresses every dishonesty that Satan can and will throw at you. But most importantly, we must remember that with God, we will have victory over Satan.

> "Submit yourselves, then, to God. Resist the devil, and he will flee from you." (James 4:7)

So what do we have to do to fight against this liar, is to know and understand his lies...we must realize that our enemy does not fight fair...He has no rules.

– Rev. Dr. Stewart Poullard

23

I Am Not Worthy

We hear that phrase expressed in many ways, though usually not in those exact words. We receive and have to live with the snide comments at work, the sarcastic remarks and even the cheap shots in our own homes. Unfortunately, one of the methods people use to feel better about themselves is to denigrate another, and often the receiver of the offence is someone close to them.

Hearing those disparaging words though, is not as bad as the feelings we allow them to invoke inside of us. Feelings of insecurity and unworthiness and being undeserving permeate our existence and bleed into all areas of our lives. And the saddest part is that they couldn't be further from the truth.

God loves you, the Creator of the universe sent His Son to die for YOU — that alone makes you more precious than anything in the world. Don't let the sin of the world bring you down. Satan will lie to you and tell you that you are not good enough — don't listen to him, and don't lie to yourself.

Know and believe that you have worth because you were made in the image of God and to be who you are. Don't give into your insecurities!

Right here, right now, no matter what is happening in your life, God loves you unconditionally. He always has, and He always will.

"You are precious in My sight. You are honored and I love you." (Isaiah 43:4)

You aren't loved because you're valuable. You're valuable because God loves you.

– Anonymous

24

The Bible Is Too Confusing

Though there is much in the Bible that is straight forward, like 'do not steal' or 'do not commit adultery', there are many verses and ideas that can be confusing.

Confusion is a dilemma that flows from a lack of understanding and an inability to see a way out. A man has been given directions to a desired location, makes a wrong turn or two and then becomes confused and disoriented as to his location. The confusion arises from a lack of understanding of the road configuration and ignorance of his current location. Of course, we know how to remedy the situation – use the right tools, including a map (or a GPS) and a street sign.

As we read the Bible, we can learn God's truths and the directions for a blessed life. But God does not leave us to our own devices; He provides us with the ability to see the truths He deems appropriate for us at just the right time. In other words, God not only holds the map and the street sign, He created them. Don't be concerned that you won't understand, but have faith that He will give you the discernment to understand the applicable verses when you most need them.

> "For the word of God is alive and active. Sharper than any double-edged sword, it penetrates even to dividing soul and spirit, joints and marrow; it judges the thoughts and attitudes of the heart." (Hebrews 4:12)

Reading the Bible without meditating on it is like trying to eat without swallowing.

— Anonymous

25

Churches Are Full Of Hypocrites!

Unfortunately, that is true. You can recognize them by their "Do as I say, not as I do" attitude. Some people have the ability to act out this character flaw without even realizing what they're doing. For example, we know that stealing, even small things, is unethical and sinful; but say a woman who claims to be a Christian gets in line for the buffet after church. She hasn't paid, but no one questions her rightful place in line. She is making a choice to steal food, while purporting to be a Christian. Do her actions make her less of a Christian? No, her salvation, if made in earnest, is secure. Does it make her a hypocrite? Yes, it does.

Now let's take a look at an observer of this situation. Frank observes her unethical behavior, considers the woman's actions, and, as expected, reacts negatively. He probably feels outraged, compounded by the realization that she is getting away with it. He may also be frustrated that he has to pay for his meal, while she doesn't. Then, bitterness could set in because of his sense of injustice.

Frank's thoughts are focused on the perpetrator and elicit his emotional reaction. The reality is that people are flawed and will continually disappoint us if we make them the center of our attention.

Now, let's assume that Frank views this woman through God's eyes. Frank would assuredly feel compassion for the woman because of her inability to turn away from this obvious immoral behavior. He would also feel thankful that God has provided him a job and money so that he is able to pay for his own food.

Diverting our focus from people to God allows us to have a positive and caring attitude toward the supposed hypocrites, as opposed to the negativity that comes from seeing and condemning others. We will be well served to keep our eyes off people and their behaviors and put them rightly where they belong — on Christ, the perfect example of how to live.

> "Judge not, and ye shall not be judged: condemn not, and ye shall not be condemned: forgive, and ye shall be forgiven." (Luke 6:37)

Always forgive your enemies — nothing annoys them so much.
– Oscar Wilde

26

Don't Worry About Me And God – We Have It Worked Out

Rob bought a new vacuum cleaner that comes with "Some Assembly Required."

This, of course, is nothing new to Rob, as he considers himself to be quite handy. The directions are easy, understandable and to the point. Instead of following the instructions, however, Rob tosses them aside because of his confidence in his superior skills.

He has laid out all the parts in front of him, takes a good look around at the challenge before him and goes to work. Every nut and bolt is placed in its corresponding position and every piece fits like a glove. The shock Rob experiences when he plugs it in and it fails to work is evident in his expression. He knew he had assembled the pieces perfectly and was befuddled as to why it wasn't working. The problem — there was a simple but essential task in the instructions that he hadn't taken as it was not evident in the parts available - he assumed he knew what he was doing. Rob threw out the instructions, thinking his plan would be good enough.

A lot of us make the same mistake when it comes to God. We think we've got everything figured out and don't need to follow God's instructions. But God doesn't have a different plan concerning eternity for different people. It's a one-size-fits-all plan that is sufficient for everyone. And it is straightforward:

"For God so loved the world that he gave his one and only Son, that whoever believes in him shall not perish but have eternal life". (John 3:16)

God loves you, and yes, He does have it worked out, but you have to be on board with His plan. And to do that, you just need to follow the proper instructions.

Without the assistance of that Divine Being ... I cannot succeed. With that assistance, I cannot fail.
– Abraham Lincoln.

27

Does God Speak To Us?

The quick answer is yes, God speaks to us. But that isn't the real issue. A better question is: When God speaks, do I listen?

God speaks to us in many ways. We can pray about something and God's response could be as blatant as receiving the opportune phone call at just the right time. But God's answer may also be as subtle as a Bible verse we read a week later or even advice from a friend months from now.

How does God speak to us? He can speak to us through his Word, the Bible. He can also speak to us through fellow Christians. And after a person commits his or her life to follow Christ, He speaks to us through the Holy Spirit who lives in us. It may feel as if you hear a whisper in your ear when no one else is around.

Expecting God to speak to you is most of the battle — the rest of the battle is believing that He will do what He says. Expect God to respond, and then, when He does, have the confidence to act accordingly.

> "In the past God spoke to our ancestors through the prophets at many times and in various ways, 2 but in these last days he has spoken to us by his Son . . ." (Hebrews 1:1-2a)

The only time my prayers are never answered is on the golf course.
— Billy Graham

28

God's Blessings

As parents, just like our parents before us, we innately want to provide blessings for our children. They have needs that we fulfill but many of us strive to go the extra mile as well – and sometimes we go hundreds of extra miles.

Toys, the latest video games and fashions, even cars and prestigious colleges are all extras that we attempt to provide. But we don't limit our efforts to material items. We teach, counsel and support them logically, spiritually and emotionally. We want our children to lead blessed lives, and who is better suited to help them than their parents? The same is true with God.

> "If you, then, though you are evil, know how to give good gifts to your children, how much more will your Father in heaven give good gifts to those who ask Him!" (Matthew 7:11)

The 'good gifts' aren't confined to the physical. God showers us with His transmissible attributes so we can be blessed: compassion, love, comfort and guidance, to name a few. He loves us more than we can imagine and is faithful to deliver His goodness to us abundantly.

> "Come, you that are blessed by my Father, inherit the kingdom prepared for you from the foundation of the world." (Matthew 25:34)

If you took the love of all the best mothers and fathers who ever lived (think about that for a moment) — all the goodness, kindness, patience, fidelity, wisdom, tenderness, strength and love — and united all those virtues in one person, that person would only be a faint shadow of the love and mercy in the heart of God for you and me.

– Brennan Manning

29

Christ's Example

Christ lived the perfect life while here on Earth and exuded His character in His actions and words. Consider a few of Christ's qualities:

- Jesus showed His love towards social outcasts, by going completely against culture and fraternizing with a prostitute.

- Jesus showed His love in feeding the hungry people.

- Jesus demonstrated His caring nature when, as He was dying on the cross, He showed concern for his mother.

- Jesus showed His compassion in healing the beloved servant of a Roman soldier.

- Jesus showed forgiveness to Peter who denied knowing him Him.

- Jesus was angered by religious hypocrites.

Christ provided us the perfect example of how to live. But will we ever achieve perfection on Earth? No, of course not but we will certainly be blessed as we strive to follow His example. Anyway, God is more concerned with the state of our hearts and also our efforts to make the right choices. For example, are we trying to love our neighbors like we love ourselves?

"And be ye kind one to another, tenderhearted, forgiving one another, even as God for Christ's sake hath forgiven you." (Ephesians 4:32)

Thankfully, we don't have to worry about being perfect. There's only been one perfect Man and they killed him on a cross.
— Unknown

30
....

My Grandmother Would Turn Over In Her Grave If I Went To That Church!

Traditions are something that we all are familiar with and typically enjoy. Many of the traditions we hold dear are accompanied by comforting memories of family and friends.

The converse is true as well. Changing traditions can make us uncomfortable, even anxious, especially if these changes are not greeted warmly by those we love and respect.

Friends and family can have negative reactions when we try to break away from the way we've always done things, and the emotions that rise in us in response can be painful. We may even dwell on the departed, and recoil at the reactions we imagine they would have. Often, we decide that breaking free from tradition is more trouble than it's worth.

But take a moment to think deeply about those who truly care for you and love you. Would they be more concerned with you and your fulfillment, or with the keeping of tradition? Imagine the roles reversed — what do you want for the people you care most about?

Think of it this way: If reaching for the fullness of God's blessings requires you to take a new path, one that departs from the ways of the past, isn't that a path you should be encouraged to take?

Is God calling you in a new direction? Are you better

served to follow God, with all His blessings and gift of eternal life, or family traditions?

"And if it seem evil unto you to serve the LORD, choose you this day whom ye will serve; ... but as for me and my house, we will serve the LORD." (Joshua 24:15)

Tradition with all its happy assumptions and necessary evils, all of its content majorities and stout killers is not always a reliable guide.

— Matthew Scully

31
. . . .

All I Need Is To Be A Good Person

"Good" is a relative term. The captain of the local 8th grade girls' travel basketball team is a good player, but she's no Kobe Bryant. The freshman scholar at Yale is a good scientist but he's not in the same stratosphere as Edison.

So what does a "good" person look like? He lies only a little, she cheats only once a year? They take the Lord's name in vain just a couple times a week? Being a "good" person is a worthy goal, but we can never be good enough to counteract all of our sins.

And that's OK, because God created a path for us to heaven that relieves us from having to worry about whether we are good enough.

> "But God commendeth his love toward us, in that, while we were yet sinners, Christ died for us." (Romans 5:8)

If people did have the ability to be "good" enough, this would negate the necessity of Christ! If spending eternity in heaven is solely dependent on what we do, how we act and what we say, then why would Christ be necessary? If you believe in God and Jesus, His son, then it can't be about what we do while we are here on earth. If that were the case, then God would have sent Jesus to die that horrendous death on the cross for nothing.

Being saved from the ill effects of our sin and spending eternity in heaven rather than hell is a free gift from God.

No matter what we have done, He is worthy of our faith and willing to forgive us if we accept His plan.

> "... for I came not to judge the world, but to save the world." (John 12:47)

Our sins alienate us from God and doom us to eternal punishment. Since we have sinned against God, only God can declare the basis on which the sins will be forgiven. We are powerless by ourselves to remove the consequences of sin (no matter how good we are)

– GospelWay.com

32
....

Christians Are Some Of The Most Judgmental People I Know!

What does God expect of us when it comes to judging others? He expects us to follow Christ's example, which is to be discerning of right and wrong, but not be condemning.

Christ hung out with the dregs of society — sinners, prostitutes and tax collectors, who at the time were known to be the least scrupulous members of their community. Christ's instruction to us was straightforward: "Love one another." People who identify themselves as Christians and yet act as if they are above the very people God instructed us to love are not following the example of Christ; they are sinning.

Judgment brings judgment upon us, Christ told us:

> "For in the same way you judge others, you will be judged, and with the measure you use, it will be measured to you." (Matthew 7:2)

That should be a scary thought for everyone, especially Christians. To be holy is one thing; to be holier than thou is quite another.

God asks us to be caring and gentle in our attitudes toward others. The Christian who treats others harshly or with indifference is not acting with God's favor.

The solution is to keep our eyes on God, for His is the only example that we ought always to follow. Don't let the sinful attitudes of others keep you from living the blessed life God has planned for you.

> "A new commandment I give you, love one another; as I have loved you, so you must love one another." (John 13:34)

It is well, when judging a friend, to remember that he is judging you with the same godlike and superior impartiality.
— Arnold Bennett

33
....

Christians Have An Entitlement Attitude

The truth is that Christians can act as wretched on the outside as everyone else.

Remember what you read from Romans?

> "For all have sinned, and come short of the glory of God." (Romans 3:23)

The key word, in this context, is "all." All have sinned — not one person stands above another when it comes to worthiness of God's grace. A Christian is no more or less entitled than anyone else, and should not act as if he is. What makes a Christian different is faith in Christ and his commitment to follow God's path toward His eternal destination. No one is entitled to God's blessings or a relationship with Him, or to spend eternity in heaven. Salvation is a gift from God, and He intends for everyone to receive it.

Sometimes Christians can appear as if they feel entitled, but it is more the confidence that comes from faith that God will take care of them. This confidence is a great and comforting thing when we are going through difficult times, but Christians should be careful not to misrepresent the source of their strength and outlook.

> "Bear with each other and forgive one another if any of you has a grievance against someone. Forgive as the Lord forgave you." (Colossians 3:13)

Our response shouldn't be pride or condemnation when we recognize someone else's sin, but rather to understand it for what it is, put it in its rightful place behind us and concentrate on God and His good intentions.

Though beauty gives you a weird sense of entitlement, it's rather frightening and threatening to have others ascribe such importance to something you know you're just renting for a while.
– Candice Bergen

34

Hell

We're all familiar with the word 'hell', but it's a safe bet that we rarely contemplate the actual place. Most of the time, we use hell as profanity or to describe an uncomfortable situation, as in "she's hell to work for" or "I'm in relationship hell."

There are also plenty of jokes about hell. One of the most popular is the idea that a man has no problem going to hell because that's where all his friends will be.

The term 'hell' is used somewhat flippantly and usually with little or no regard to the reality of the destination. Unfortunately, hell is very real and a very serious matter.

As punishment for his rebellion, God prepared hell for Satan and his demons. It is a terrible place, full of torment, eternal fire and a thirst that is never quenched.

> "They will throw them into the blazing furnace, where there will be weeping and gnashing of teeth." (Matthew 13:42)

> "They will be punished with everlasting destruction and shut out from the presence of the Lord and from the glory of His might." (2 Thessalonians 1:9)

But take heart!! God wants no one else to be there - this is the very reason He prepared a way for us to avoid the eternal suffering that Satan will endure. God wants us to live eternally with him in the paradise that is heaven.

Once you understand the stark difference between the two choices of where you could spend eternity, your choice should be easy.

He supposed that even in Hell, people got an occasional sip of water, if only so they could appreciate the full horror of unrequited thirst when it sets in again.

– Stephen King

35

Heaven

The Bible describes heaven as God's glorious dwelling place. We are given many details about Heaven, but there is one really important bit of information we need to understand so that we can live life here on earth through eternal eyes. Jesus tells us:

> "And if I go and prepare a place for you, I will come again, and receive you unto myself; that where I am, there ye may be also." (John 14:3)

This is great news for us! Jesus desires that each of us to live in heaven with Him for all of eternity.

So, what will eternity in heaven be like?

> "He will wipe every tear from their eyes. There will be no more death or mourning or crying or pain, for the old order of things has passed away." (Revelation 21:4)

God promises us that the pain and suffering we experience here on earth will be no more in heaven. And better yet, all the unpleasant memories we carry with us will disappear.

What a great way to spend eternity: no pain, no suffering and no regret!

If you are a Christian, you are not a citizen of this world trying to get to heaven. You are a citizen of heaven making your way through this world.

– Vance Havner

36
....

The Trinity: Father, Son and Holy Spirit

The "Trinity" and "Holy Trinity" are terms familiar to most adults, even if they've never been to church. Still, the idea of the "Trinity" — God the Father, God the Son, God the Holy Spirit —can be a little overwhelming to comprehend.

Here is an explanation of the Trinity in a nutshell: There is one God, but our God has three parts (persons), all with distinctive roles. God the Father created the heavens and the Earth. Jesus, the Son of God, is our Advocate and our Redeemer. The Holy Spirit is our Counselor and Comforter. Each of the Trinity is completely holy, distinct from one another, but one in the same at all times.

Think of it this way to understand the different roles each takes: You're on trial. You sit in the courtroom with your lawyer beside you, the judge is on the bench and a witness on the stand, ready to testify. You look over the stack of papers in front of you, proof of your condemnation and consider the many sins you have committed throughout your life. You know the facts of your situation — you are guilty, the lawyer will be your advocate, the witness will be truthful and the judge will hand down the dreadful verdict.

Thankfully, though, you have the Holy Trinity in your courtroom. The Holy Spirit, your lawyer, leans close to you and whispers that you are going to be all right. Jesus, in the witness stand, displays the scars on His hands and speaks on your behalf to God, the Judge. It is as if Christ is saying, "I died on the cross for him, he has declared Me as his Savior and I have made him innocent." And with that said, God smiles and with a smashing of His gavel, declares your sins forgiven!

Full understanding of the Trinity may be beyond us but the Trinity's purposes are clear.

> "May the grace of the Lord Jesus Christ, and the love of God, and the fellowship of the Holy Spirit be with you all." (2 Corinthians 13:14)

Bring me a worm that can comprehend a man, and then I will show you a man that can comprehend the Triune God.
— John Wesley

37

You WILL Live Forever!

If you're like most people, you'd rather not think about death. Just ask anyone who makes a living selling life insurance. They would tell you that encouraging someone to contemplate their own death is the hardest part of their job. Of course, as every widow knows, not thinking about it and a lack of planning for it can have devastating consequences.

Sooner or later, we're all going to die. But that is not the end of our life – just the life as we know it now.

> "The gift of God is eternal life through Jesus Christ our Lord." (Romans 6:23)

Does that literally mean we will live forever? The Bible is clear about this: Yes, we will. You. Me. Every one of us. The only question is, where?

When we purchase a gift for a friend or loved one, we hope it is pleasing and that he or she shows gratitude in response. The same is true of God. He is offering us the "gift" of eternal life in heaven with Him, and He wants and desires our joyful acceptance of it.

But He also gives us the choice of not accepting the gift - either way though, our spirit will live forever. And we all know what the alternative to heaven is. Those who reject salvation:

> ". . . will pay the penalty of eternal destruction, away from the presence of the Lord and from the glory of His power . . ." (2 Thessalonians 1:7-9)

The gateway to heaven is to accept God's gift of salvation through belief in Jesus Christ and His redeeming grace. Should we choose not to accept God's gift, we still will have eternal life — just not with God.

So, Heaven or hell - which will it be for you?

"This short life, important and significant though it may be in its setting, is no more than a prelude to a share in the timeless life of God."

– JB Phillips, "New Testament Christianity"

38

Death Is Nothingness –
No Pain, No Memory; It Won't Be So Bad

We've all heard the saying, "there are only two definite things in life – death and taxes". And though death is a difficult subject for most to contemplate, we all will experience it.

Death as we know it marks the end of our life on Earth and in our present bodies. But death is not our end, it is a new beginning.

Paul stated in II Corinthians, "We are confident, I say, and willing rather to be absent from the body, and to be present with the Lord." Paul equated being delivered out of this Earthly body, to being immediately with the Lord. We will not experience nothingness, for there absolutely is something!

> "These will go away into eternal punishment, but the righteous into eternal life." (Matthew 25:46)

Eternal life means exactly what it says it is – a life without end. Where you live that life, is up to you. God wants you to be in heaven with Him for eternity, and has prepared the way for you.

The Bible is clear about God's desires. The essential question for you is: Where do you want to spend eternity – in heaven with all the blessings and joy God has planned for you or in hell with an eternity of pain and suffering?

> "... choose you this day whom ye will serve; ... but as for me and my house, we will serve the LORD." (Joshua 24:15)

Someday you will read in the papers that Moody is dead. Don't you believe a word of it. . . . That which is born of the Spirit shall live forever.

– Dwight L. Moody

39
. . . .

What Does It Mean To Have Joy?

We all strive for happiness and to achieve those circumstances (or 'happenings') and/or events that get us there. The problem with feeling happy is that it is fleeting. Happiness comes and goes as does the events that help us attain it. These things that we obtain are but moments in time. New earrings, a new house and getting married are all happy times, but those conditions are sure to change. The earrings will probably be lost, the house is demanding on our time and finances and we all know how much effort and sometimes pain goes into marriage.

So in reality, happiness isn't all it's cracked up to be. And God didn't promise us happiness anyway! What He did promise us is oh so much better - God promised us joy!

"I have told you this so that my joy may be in you
and that your joy may be complete." (John 15:11)

Joy, unlike happiness, is a state of being. A joyful mind and spirit is not easily bent by outside influences. This doesn't mean we won't be sad at times, but the state of joyfulness that comes from God persists through periods of despair and permeates throughout our lives.

How do you become joyful? Realize that you have the Creator of the universe on your side, and if He is for you, no one and nothing can overcome you.

Happiness is not a goal; it is a by-product.
– Eleanor Roosevelt

40
....

If Getting Saved Is So Simple, You Might Ask, Then Why Not Just Wait And Do It On My Deathbed?

Let's look at it another way.

Frank isn't much of a gambler. Sure, he goes to a casino when his friends asked him to a couple of times a year and he travels to the local horseracing track during the summer, but it's not a deep need.

Knowing this, his wife asked why he bought the occasional lottery ticket when he'd stop for milk or bread at the local gas 'n sip.

He didn't see the harm, since he bought them only once or twice a month, and only when he happened to be in that store on the day of the drawing. Plus, what if God wanted him to win the lottery?

So, if you were Frank's friend and his numbers were drawn, would you encourage him to tell the lottery people that he'd like to wait 40 years before collecting his winnings, or would you want him to enjoy the benefits right away?

The same principle applies to salvation. Why not accept the free gift God has given you now — and reap the benefits of His blessings for the rest of your life? Why miss out on God's blessings for another moment?

It's true that Jesus forgave the man on the cross next to Him and told him that he would be with Him in paradise that very day — which means that you can be saved at any moment. But God knows your heart, and if you know the truth now and put it off, perhaps your heart isn't where it needs to be.

We all hope to live a long and full life, but God does not promise us tomorrow. We have only today. So, where is your heart? Will you make the decision today to accept God's free gift of salvation and have assurance that you will be joyful and blessed in this life and reside in Heaven forever after? If so, the next few pages will guide you on the most important decision you will ever make.

God's arrows of affliction are sharp and painful so He can get our attention. He won't let His beloved children get away with sin because He knows it robs us of blessings, opportunities, and even character refinement.

– Charles Stanley

We sinned for no reason but an incomprehensible lack of love, and He saved us for no reason but an incomprehensible excess of love.

– Peter Kreeft

There is never time in the future in which we will work out our salvation. The challenge is in the moment; the time is always now.

– James A. Baldwin

Appendix I
The Gospel Message, In a Nutshell

God wants very much to have a relationship with all of us while we are here on Earth, but more importantly, He wants us to be with Him for eternity in heaven.

This good news is accompanied by some bad news though. Sin is a problem. Unfortunately, we live in a world that has been filled with sin since Adam and Eve defied God in the Garden of Eden. Our sin has separated us from God because He hates sin and His holiness makes it impossible for Him to be in its presence and unfortunately, that includes us in our sinful state.

Thankfully, God put a plan in place so that we can be reconciled to Him.

> Reconciled: to "bring two or more people back into a friendly relationship with each other after a dispute or estrangement".

God wants to reconcile with us and the only way to do that is to implement a plan to take away our sin.

His plan was to send his Son, Jesus to earth, which He did, the day we celebrate as Christmas. Jesus then lived a perfect and blameless life here on Earth, showing us the perfect way to live, be and act. Then Jesus was the perfect sacrifice, dying on the cross, taking on the sin of the world for us. On the third day, He was raised, conquering Satan and sin in one magnificent event which we celebrate as Easter.

ABC's of Salvation

God has done the hard work - now it's our turn! Salvation, or being saved from an eternal life in hell, is a free gift of God but we must accept it. In order to do this, we must Admit that we are sinners. Then we must Believe the Gospel message (Jesus, born of a virgin, lived a perfect life, died a sacrificial death and rose again after three days) and that in Him alone are we able to be saved. And then we must Confess that Jesus is our Lord and Savior.

How do you receive the gift of salvation? If you believe the above, say this simple prayer:

> Dear God in Heaven: I know that I'm a sinner and I can't save myself. I believe You sent your Son Jesus to die on the cross as a sacrifice to pay the penalty for my sins. I ask Jesus to come and save me today. In Jesus name I pray, Amen.

That simple act is all you need to defeat Satan and begin a victorious life in the light and love of God.

Supporting scriptures: Romans 3:23 (all have sinned); Romans 6:23 (sin = death, free gift); Isaiah 59:2 (our separation from God); John 3:16 (God so loved the world); 1 Peter 2:24 (by His wounds we are healed); Ephesians 2:8 (by grace we are saved through faith); Romans 10:9 (confess with our mouths)

For Further Reference

Don't take our word for it!! It is my hope that you want more information on many subjects covered in this book; please seek out answers to your questions. There are many ways you can gain more understanding – study the Bible, pray, listen to a Christian radio station, speak to a Pastor or a Christian in your life and attend a Bible believing church. This is just the beginning of a journey that will last throughout eternity. May God bless you!

Topical Index

Understanding God
Daily Entry: 5, 6, 9, 12, 13, 15, 19, 20, 27, 28, 29, 36, 39

God V. Religion
Daily Entry: 1, 2, 4

Understanding Flawed Christians
Daily Entry: 14, 25, 29, 32, 33

Understanding the Bible
Daily Entry: 3, 7, 8, 17, 24, 40

Understanding Eternity
Daily Entry: 34, 35, 37, 38

Understanding Satan
Daily Entry: 21, 22, 23

Common Misconceptions
Daily Entry: 4, 7, 8, 10, 13, 16, 19, 23, 26, 30, 31

Faith
Daily Entry: 3, 5, 11, 12, 16, 18, 28, 40

Character Issues
Daily Entry: 7, 8, 16, 31

Sources

1. Poe, Edgar Allen. "Find Quotes." *Good Reads*. Web. January 12, 2015. https://www.goodreads.com/quotes/search?utf8=%E2%9C%93&q=religion%2C+poe&commit=Search

2. Franklin, Benjamin. "Calvinist Protestant Theology in American Political Thought." *All Academic, Inc,*. Web. January 16, 2015. http://citation.allacademic.com/meta/p_mla_apa_research_citation/0/6/2/9/2/pages62923/p62923-

3. Lincoln, Abraham. *Search Quotes. Web.* January 16, 2015. http://www.searchquotes.com/quotation/I_believe_the_Bible_is_the_best_gift_God_has_ever_given_to_man._All_the_good_from_the_Savior_of_the_/362841/

4. Roosevelt, Franklin, D. "Franklin D. Roosevelt Quotes." *ThinkExist.com*. Web. January 16, 2015. http://thinkexist.com/quotation/rules_are_not_necessarily_sacred-principles_are/152433.html

5. "Declaration of Independence" (US 1776).

6. Edwards, Jonathan. "The Peace Which Christ Gives His True Followers." *BibleBB.com*. Tony Capoccia. Web. January 16, 2015. http://www.biblebb.com/files/edwards/peace2.htm

7. Moody, Dwight L. "Encouraging and Inspiring Quotes from Dwight L. Moody." *Kevin Halloran*. Web. January 16, 2015. http://www.kevinhalloran.net/d-l-moody-quotes/

8. Bunyan, John. *The Pilgrim's Progress*. Vol. XV, Part 1. The Harvard Classics. New York: P.F. Collier & Son, 1909–14; Bartleby.com, 2001. www.bartleby.com/15/1/.

9. Columbus, Christopher. "Christopher Columbus Quotes." *Brainy Quotes*. Web. January 16, 2015. http://www.brainyquote.com/quotes/authors/c/christopher_columbus.html

10. Warfield, Benjamin B. "Benjamin Warfield Quotes." *oChristian.com*. Web. January 16, 2015. http://christian-quotes.ochristian.com/B.B.-Warfield-Quotes/

11. Moody, DL. *Search Quotes. Web.* January 17, 2015. http://www.searchquotes.com/quotation/If_God_is_your_partner,_make_your_plans_BIG!/362179/

12. Spurgeon, Charles. *The Spurgeon Archive*. Web. January 18, 2015. www.spurgeon.org/mainpage.htm

13. Backcus, William. *Daily Christian Quotes*. Web. January 18, 2015. http://dailychristianquote.com/william-backcus/

14. Sunday, Billy. "Billy Sunday Quotes." *Brainy Quote*. Web. January 18, 2015. http://www.brainyquote.com/quotes/authors/b/billy_sunday.html?vm=l

15. Lincoln, Abraham. "Abraham Lincoln Quotes." *ThinkExist.com*. Web. January 19, 2015. http://thinkexist.com/quotation/i_have_always_found_that_mercy_bears_richer/222587.html

16. Stott, John R. W, "John R. W. Stott Quotes." *ThinkExist.com*. Web. January 19, 2015. http://thinkexist.com/quotes/john_r.w._stott/

17. Greeley, Horace. *Good Reads*. Web. January 19, 2015. http://www.goodreads.com/quotes/117998-it-is-impossible-to-enslave-mentally-or-socially-a-bible-reading

18. King, Martin Luther, Jr. "Martin Luther King, Jr. Quotes*.*" *Brainy Quote*. Web. January 19, 2015. http://www.brainyquote.com/quotes/quotes/m/martinluth105087.html

19. Socrates. "Socrates Quotes*".* *Brainy Quote*. Web. January 19, 2015. http://www.brainyquote.com/quotes/quotes/s/socrates107382.html

20. Paddock, Graham. "Why Fear God?" *Fear God*. Graham Barker. Web. January 20, 2015. http://www.feargod.net/fear.php

21. King, Gary H. "Quotes About Prayer." *Quote Garden*. Web. January 20, 2015. http://www.quotegarden.com/prayer.html

22. Poullard, Rev. Dr. Stewart. *"*Satan Quotes*.". Brainy Quote*. Web. January 20, 2015. http://www.brainyquote.com/quotes/keywords/satan.html

23. Anonymous

24. Anonymous

25. Wilde, Oscar. "Forgiveness." *Books.Google*. Mira Balanchandran. Web. January 20, 2015. https://books.google.com/books?id=1siBQAAQBAJ&pg=PA44&dq=Always+forgive+your+enemies+%E2%80%94+nothing+annoys+them+so+much.++%E2%80%93+Oscar+Wilde&hl=en&sa=X&ei=60VOXHIZL7sATRgoLQCQ&ved=0CB8Q6AEwAA#v=onepage&q=Always%20forgive%20your%20enemies%20%E2%80%94%20nothing%20annoys%20them%20so%20much.%20%20%E2%80%93%20Oscar%20Wilde&f=false

26. Lincoln, Abraham. "Abraham Quotable Quotes." *Good Reads*. Web. January 19, 2015. http://www.goodreads.com/quotes/715317-without-the-assistance-of-that-divine-being-i-cannot-succeed

27. Graham, Billy. "Billy Graham Quotes*."* *Brainy Quote*. Web. January 21, 2015. http://www.brainyquote.com/quotes/quotes/b/billygra-

ha105405.html

28. Manning, Brennan. "Brennan Manning." *Pinterest*. Web. January 22, 2015. http://www.pinterest.com/april_dawn0625/brennan-manning/

29. *Anonymous*

30. Scully, Matthew. *Good Reads*. Web. January 21, 2015. https://www.goodreads.com/quotes/326141-tradition-with-all-its-happy-assumptions-and-necessary-evils-all

31. "Jesus as Your Savior." *Gospel Way*. Web. January 22, 2015. http://www.gospelway.com/god/jesus-savior.php

32. Bennett, Arnold. "Arnold Bennett Quotes." Brainy Quote. Web. January 22, 2015. http://www.brainyquote.com/quotes/authors/a/arnold_bennett.html

33. Bergen, Candice. "Candice Bergen Quotes". *Brainy Quote*. Web. January 22, 2015. http://www.brainyquote.com/quotes/quotes/c/candiceber359690.html

34. King, Stephen. "Full Dark, No Stars Quotes." *Good Reads*. Web. January 22, 2015. http://www.goodreads.com/work/quotes/11067830-full-dark-no-stars

35. Havner, Vance. "Vance Havner Quotes." *Good Reads*. Web. January 22, 2015. http://www.goodreads.com/author/show/249386.Vance_Havner

36. *Wesley, John.* "John Wesley Quote – 5 Ways the Trinity Reveals God's Love." *Christian Quotes*. Web. January 22, 2015. http://www.christianquotes.info/images/john-wesley-quote-5-ways-trinity-reveals-gods-love/#ixzz3Pc5OWqqN

37. Phillips, JB. *JB Phillips Translation of the New Testament*. Web. January 25, 2015. http://www.ccel.org/bible/phillips/JBPhillips.htm

38. Moody, Dwight L. "DL Moody Quotes." *ThinkExist.com*. Web. January 25, 2015. http://thinkexist.com/quotes/dwight_l._moody/

39. Roosevelt, Eleanor. *Good Reads*. Web. January 25, 2015. http://www.goodreads.com/author/quotes/44566.Eleanor_Roosevelt

40. Stanley, Charles. "Charles Stanley Quotes." *Brainy Quotes*. Web. January 25, 2015. http://www.brainyquote.com/quotes/authors/c/charles_stanley.html

Bible Versions

Holy Bible: New International Version. (2011). Grand Rapids, Mich.: Zondervan

Peterson, Eugene H. The Message. Bible Gateway. Web. 25 Oct. 2012.

You Version – "A free Bible on your phone, tablet, and computer. YouVersion is a simple, ad-free Bible that brings God's Word into your daily life." www.youversion.com

About the Author

Beverly Swimm is a first-time author, having edited several published books for others. Beverly was born and raised in Lexington, KY, and has lived most of her adult life in upstate New York. She has been involved in various ministries including children's choral direction, drama director, small group leader and Bible story teller. She currently attends Grace Fellowship Church in Halfmoon, NY. Bev was inspired by the Holy Spirit to write this book as a means to give to others understanding of faith, God, and the blessings to be had from a relationship with Him. When she's not working or spending time with her children Katie, Tommy, Joshua and Holly, Beverly enjoys a variety of activities, in addition to being an avid tennis player.

For more information on her ministry, Seek and Find, visit her website at www.SeekandFindMinistry.org and you can follow her on Twitter @LuvsGodnCountry.